Words for the Advent & Christmas Season

by
Bishop Hugh Gilbert, OSB

All booklets are published thanks to the generous support of the members of the Catholic Truth Society

CATHOLIC TRUTH SOCIETY
PUBLISHERS TO THE HOLY SEE

Contents

 First published 2014 by The Incorporated Catholic Truth Society, 40-46 Harleyford Road London SE11 5AY Tel: 020 7640 0042 Fax: 020 7640 0046.

ISBN 978 1 78469 007 6

Introduction

The liturgical year - with its Sundays and weekdays, Easter and Christmas, Advent and Lent, ferias and feasts - is one of the great givens of the Christian life. We live our lives within it. This is true even when we are not consciously averting to it. It's a framework, a mould, a supporting rhythm, a background that at some peak times becomes the foreground. It has, too, been one of the great facts of European and Western cultural history. We're familiar with the civil year (which comes to us from the Romans), the financial year, the academic year... But there is this other presence too - still hanging on even in semi-pagan Britain - and every revolutionary attempt to conjure it away (1789, 1917) has itself foundered.

In the Roman rite now, we have a liturgical year both luminously intent on the essentials and rich in its details. "By means of the yearly cycle", says the *Calendarium Romanum* of 1969, echoing Vatican II's *Sacrosanctum Concilium*, "the Church celebrates the whole mystery of Christ, from his Incarnation until the day of Pentecost and the expectation of his coming again." Central is the Easter Triduum - from the evening Mass of Maundy Thursday to the Compline of Easter Sunday. Out of this flows the Easter season, with its fifty days culminating in Pentecost, and towards it flows the critical season of Lent. Such is the "Easter cycle".

Second to it in stature is the "Christmas cycle", with its similar pattern of a season of celebration, running to the feast of the Lord's Baptism, and a season of preparation, much-cherished Advent. There is the fine Byzantine phrase for all this: "the winter Pasch".

Immaculate Conception of the Blessed Virgin Mary

Cut off from God, we die

"Come, Lord Jesus! Come, and save us! Come and set us free!" This is what we pray in Advent. We call on Christ to come and save us. Christ saves us from two things, sin and death.

Sin is turning away from God. "Where are you?" God asks Adam. He's no longer in the place God had set him. He's no longer, in a sense, visible to God. He's not in his presence. "I was afraid because I was naked, so I hid". He had gone into hiding. This is sin. Sin disconnects from God. It's like taking the plug out of the wall and losing the flow of electricity. Disconnect a laptop from the mains and it will run for a while on its battery. But in the end the battery will die. The screen will blank. And access to the internet will be lost. There'll be no more communication with others. Or imagine our planet stopped orbiting the sun. It would just spin away into darkness. If we turn away from God, if we lose sight of him, we start to lose sight of ourselves and others, something starts to collapse inside us. We fragment. We revert to chaos. We're no longer ourselves. We fall out with others. We find ourselves alone. Eventually we implode. And death - going into the dark - is a kind of outward sign of all of this. It's the last working out of sin.

Jesus comes to save us from death

"Come, Lord Jesus! Come and save us!"

Our Lord has come. He does come. He will come. He comes to reconnect us. "Blessed be God the Father of our Lord Jesus Christ ... Before the world was made, he chose us, chose us in Christ, to be holy and spotless, and to live through love in his presence". "And the Lord God called to him, 'Where are you?'" Our Lord comes to take us out of hiding and into the presence of his Father. He comes to connect us again. He makes us one again in ourselves, and with one another. The electricity of grace flows into us, the screen lights up with the light of faith, we can connect with others (charity). He comes to form a new network, a new humanity, his mystical Body. And so taking away our sin, he takes away our death. We will still physically die - the old world has to run its course in each of us - but dying in Christ is a passing over to eternal happiness in the communion of saints, and that eternal happiness will be completed at the end of time by the resurrection of the body. As St Bernard put it:

"Christ takes possession of the whole man (person): he created the whole man, he redeemed the whole man and he will glorify the whole man."

In Mary, her Son anticipates our salvation

And so, like the angel in the Gospel, we come to Mary. And we say, "Hail, full of grace, the Lord is with you." By the eternal will of the eternal Father what he wants to do in all of us, he does first of all and most of all, most clearly of all, in Mary, the predestined Mother of his Son.

Our Lord saves us from sin and from death. And first of all and most of all, most radiantly of all, he saves Mary, his Mother and the Image of the Church. So in Advent, in the cold and dark, we celebrate her Immaculate Conception, her salvation from sin. It's God's spring in the middle of Nature's winter, a sign winter is already deeply defeated. And in August, at the height of summer, we feast her Assumption, her victory over death. Christ saves us from sin through the Cross, he saves us from death through his Resurrection. And it's in Mary, first of all and most of all, that Jesus's Cross and Resurrection work their magic, have their full effect, do their job. "It is finished / accomplished" were Jesus's last words on the Cross. And his Mother was standing by.

In every saint, in the good and holy people we know, and in Mary first and most of all, we see the salvation of God. We see God's plan for us, what we are called to be, what the Church is: humanity no longer in hiding but living through love in his presence. "Behold the handmaid of the Lord; let it be done to me according to your word."

God wants to bring his marvels to completion in us too

"Come, Lord Jesus! Come and save us!" The Advent prayer is answered already today.

Mary was preserved from original sin from her very conception. She received the Holy Spirit, the fruit of Christ's Paschal mystery. She was clothed with the garments of salvation. In her God the Father, the God of Abraham, Isaac and Jacob answered the long yearnings of Israel to be pure, to stand before God, to be his holy people. In her he built the Temple he would fill with the presence of his Son. He placed her already, unawares, in Christ, so that when the angel came with the message of the Incarnation, she would be ready. When the heavens would look down, the earth would open up. There would be a perfect receptivity. And so the door of faith - *porta fidei* - did indeed swing open. "Behold the handmaid of the Lord; let it be done to me according to your word."

The marvels God works in Mary, he is working in us, and wants to more and more. The one plan of God the

Father, the one death and resurrection of Christ, the one Holy Spirit involves, embraces, overshadows Mary and each and all of us. We are all caught up in the same epic of grace, the same love story. We shouldn't think of Mary as remote, set on a pedestal. She's at the heart of things. She's the most connected of us all because she's the most redeemed. She's very close. Her salvation from sin and death is like a great space we can enter too, and there in our measure receive the same grace.

She's in heaven. We are on earth, still struggling along. But together with her, and with the whole Advent Church, we cry out, "Come Lord Jesus! Come and save us!", completely confident we'll be heard.

Advent - a Time for Silence

God speaks to us in silence

We live in a noisy world. Our towns and cities are full of noise. There is noise in the skies and on the roads. There is noise in our homes, and even in our churches. And most of all there is noise in our minds and hearts.

The Danish philosopher Kierkegaard once wrote: "The present state of the world and the whole of life is diseased. If I were a doctor and I were asked for my advice, I should reply: 'Create silence! Bring people to silence!' The Word of God cannot be heard in the noisy world of today. And even if it were trumpeted forth with all the panoply of noise so that it could be heard in the midst of all the other noise, then it would no longer be the Word of God. Therefore, create silence!"

"Create silence!" There's a challenge here. Surely speaking is a good and healthy thing? Yes indeed. Surely there are bad kinds of silence? Yes again. But still Kierkegaard is on to something.

There is a simple truth at stake. There can be no real relationship with God, there can be no real meeting with God, without silence. Silence prepares for that meeting and silence follows it. An early Christian wrote, "To someone who has experienced Christ himself, silence is more precious than anything else." For us God has the first word, and our silence opens our hearts to hear him. Only then will our own words really be words, echoes of God's, and not just more litter on the rubbish dump of noise.

The stillness of Christmas

"How silently, how silently, the wondrous gift is given." So the carol goes. For all the noise, rush and rowdiness of contemporary Christmasses, we all know there is a link between Advent and silence, Christmas and silence. Our cribs are silent places. Who can imagine Mary as a noisy person? In the Gospels, St Joseph never says a word; he simply obeys the words brought him by angels. And when John the Baptist later comes out with words of fire, it is after years of silence in the desert. Add to this the silence of our long northern nights, and the silence that follows the snow. Isn't all this asking us to still ourselves?

A passage from the Old Testament Book of Wisdom describes the night of Israel's Exodus from Egypt as a night full of silence. It is used by the liturgy of the night of Jesus's birth:

> "When a deep silence covered all things and night was in the middle of its course, your all-powerful Word, O Lord, leapt from heaven's royal throne" (*Ws* 18:14-15).

"Holy night, silent night!" So we sing. The outward silence of Christmas night invites us to make silence within us. Then the Word can leap into us as well, as a wise man wrote: "If deep silence has a hold on what is inside us, then into us too the all-powerful Word will slip quietly from the Father's throne."

This is the Word who proceeds from the silence of the Father. He became an infant, and "infant" means literally "one who doesn't speak". The child Jesus would have cried - for air and drink and food - but he didn't speak. "Let him who has ears to hear, hear what this loving and mysterious silence of the eternal Word says to us." We need to listen to this quietness of Jesus, and allow it to make its home in our minds and hearts.

A sanctuary where the Christ child can be born

"Create silence!" How much we need this! The world needs places, oases, sanctuaries, of silence.

And here comes a difficult question: what has happened to silence in our churches? Many people ask this. When the late Canon Duncan Stone, as a young priest in the 1940s, visited a parish in the Highlands, he was struck often to find thirty or forty people kneeling there in silent prayer. Now often there is talking up to the very beginning of Mass, and it starts again immediately afterwards. But what is a church for, and why do we go there? We go to meet the Lord and the Lord comes to meet us. "The Lord is in his holy temple. Let all the earth keep silence before him!" said the prophet Habakkuk. Surely the silent sacramental presence of the Lord in the tabernacle should lead us to silence? We need to focus ourselves and put aside distractions before the Mass begins. We want to prepare to hear the word of the Lord in the readings and homily. Surely we need a quiet mind to connect to the great Eucharistic Prayer? And when we receive Holy Communion, surely we want to listen to what the Lord God has to say, "the voice that speaks of peace"? Being together in this way can make us one - the Body of Christ - quite as effectively as words.

The courtesy of silence

A wise elderly priest of the diocese said recently, "Two people talking stop forty people praying."

"Create silence!" I don't want to be misunderstood. Babies will be babies, and toddlers toddlers. Nor are we meant to come and go from church as cold isolated individuals, uninterested in one another. We want our parishes to be warm and welcoming places. We want to meet and greet and speak with one another. There are arrangements to be made, items of news to be shared, messages to be passed. A good word is above the best gift, says the Bible. But it is a question of where and when. Better in the porch than at the back of the church. Better after the Mass in a hall or a room. There is a time and place for speaking and a time and place for silence. In the church itself, so far as possible, silence should prevail. It should be the norm before and after Mass, and at other times as well. When there is a real need to say something, let it be done as quietly as can be. At the very least, such silence is a courtesy towards those who want to pray. It signals our reverence for the Blessed Sacrament. It respects the longing of the Holy Spirit to prepare us to celebrate the sacred mysteries. And then the Mass, with its words and music and movement and its own moments of silence, will become more real. It will unite us at a deeper level, and those who visit our churches will sense the Holy One amongst us.

"Create silence!" It is an imperative. May the Word coming forth from silence find our silence waiting for him like a crib! "The devil," said St Ambrose, "loves noise; Christ looks for silence".

Advent - a Time of Hope

A childlike virtue

Advent is a time of *hope*. Advent culminates in Christmas, in the birth of a child. And what gives so much hope as the birth of a child?

Hope is a need today. Many say that. Timothy Radcliffe begins his book on *What is the Point of being a Christian* with hope. Pope John Paul II was called a *Witness to Hope*, and wrote *Crossing the Threshold of Hope*. Pope Benedict dedicated his second Encyclical to hope. And these are only voices in a wider chorus of thoughtful people, not all of them Christian.

Almost too familiar here is the image of the French poet Charles Péguy (1873-1914): the little girl hope between her two big adult sisters, Faith and Charity. But let me quote nonetheless:

"On the uphill path, sandy and troublesome,
On the uphill road.
Dragged along, hanging from the arms
of her two older sisters,

Who hold her by the hand,
The little hope,
Pushes on.
And in between her two older sisters she seems to let herself be carried.
Like a child who lacks the energy to walk.
And is dragged along the road in spite of herself.
But in reality it is she who moves the other two.
And who carries them,
And who moves the whole world.
And who carries it.
Because no one ever works except for children.
And the two older ones don't walk except
for the youngest."

Another, not so other, image for hope comes from Emily Dickinson (1830-1886):

"Hope is the thing with feathers
That perches in the soul,
And sings the tune without the words,
And never stops at all,

And sweetest in the gale is heard;
And sore must be the storm
That could abash the little bird
That kept so many warm" (*Hope* I).

"And sings the tune without the words" - that is profound indeed. And fine too is the simple line, "And never stops at all." Isn't the irrepressible capacity for hope, hope against hope, the most heartbreakingly beautiful thing in the human being?

I once heard Stefan Vanistendael speak about the concept of "resilience": the capacity of the human being to bounce back. And that too was in the context of children. The real "inner child" is hope.

The true hope for adults in our time

In October 1999, a Special Assembly of the Synod of Bishops for Europe was held in Rome, and almost four years later, in June 2003, John Paul II published the Apostolic Exhortation, which was intended as a summing-up, *Ecclesia in Europa*. And "hope" became the central message of all this. The Holy Spirit can be with Bishops as well as poets. We must believe that! I feel there is a touch of the Spirit here in offering as diagnosis of Europe's current metaphysical ills a loss of hope, and as cure its reviviscence. *"Throughout the Synod, a powerful impulse towards hope gradually became evident"* (4).

Europe needs hope - true, not illusory hope, and we as European Christians need it too. We can feel hopeless about the prospects of the Church. Every human being needs to resist the demon of despondency and despair. Perhaps the need for hope grows with the years: the middle-aged need it more than the young (who sometimes have it in abundance), and the elderly more than the middle-aged (who can at least envisage themselves still doing things).

Two New Testament texts come in here: St Paul's description of the Gentiles as "having no hope and without God in the world" (*Ep* 2:12). There is the diagnosis of the pagan, and neo-pagan, condition.

St Peter's exhortation to his fellow-believers: "Have no fear, nor be troubled, but in your hearts reverence Christ as Lord. Always be prepared to make a defence to anyone who calls you to account for the hope that is in you" (*1 Pt* 3:14-15). There is the remedy.

It is good to have a sense of our responsibility, as Christians, in this particular period of history.

"Hope, O my soul, hope," said St Teresa of Avila to herself. How then can we restore hope to ourselves? I like the metaphor of the "horizon". Our Christian hope is the horizon within and towards which we live our lives. It is, as Hebrews says, "a sure and steadfast anchor of the soul, a hope that enters into the inner shrine behind the curtain" (6:19). Or again, it's the light in our eyes. It's what gives light to our eyes. To you, O Lord, I have lifted up my soul!

Hope is God's gift of life

There is the natural quality of hope, without which we can't live, we can't get up in the morning. But there is also hope the infused theological virtue, a gift of the Holy Spirit, given us in our baptism, and uniting us to God. Its object is the hope expressed in the Lord's Prayer: *Thy Kingdom come*. It includes, purifies and goes beyond our natural hopes. "Let us say once again," wrote Pope Benedict in *Spe Salvi*: "we need the greater and lesser hopes that keep us going day by day. But these are not enough without the great hope, which must surpass everything else. This great hope can only be God, who encompasses the whole of reality and who can bestow upon us what we, by ourselves, cannot attain. The fact that it comes to us as a gift is actually part of hope. God is the foundation of hope: not any god, but the God who has a human face and who has loved us to the end, each one of us and humanity in its entirety. His Kingdom is not an imaginary hereafter, situated in a future that will never arrive; his Kingdom is present wherever he is loved and wherever his love reaches us" (*SS* 31). Yes, isn't that our hope, isn't that the Kingdom: being loved by God and loving him, not without others, here and hereafter? This is the hope that nothing can take away from us. The great hope...

We can always pray for more hope. We experience redemption subjectively through the virtues of faith, hope and love. The more they fill our hearts and determine our actions, the more redeemed we will be and even "feel".

Hope is not the same as a cheerful temperament or a natural optimism. It's not the wearing of rose-tinted glasses. Hope is a choice, a decision, an act of the will. It is a chosen attitude. I can choose to be hopeful. And then, "If I live every minute perfectly, my life will be holy. The road of hope is paved with little steps of hope. The life of hope is made up of brief minutes of hope" (Abp Nguyen Van Thuan, *The Testimony of Hope* p. 52).

Hope helps us accept both disappointments and joys. Disappointments purify our hope. French has two words for hope, *espoir* and *espérance*. An *espoir* is a concrete hope, the hope, e.g., of getting a good mark in one's exams, or in getting a good job. There are many *espoirs* possible. There's a plurality here. *Espérance* is more the quality or virtue of hope. It seems to go beyond the many particular hopes we can have. It is the little bird that doesn't stop singing; it's the tune without words.

God's hope eclipses lesser hopes

Some people have distinguished ordinary, everyday hopes for definite things: money, health and so on, and another more fundamental kind of hoping which does not appear to have a precise nameable object, but which is still real. Or again, they've distinguished, "hoping that" X will happen (or not) and simply "hoping". Or again, hoping to "have" something, and - what's far less determinate - hoping to "become" or to "be" something. The objective Christian hope is addressed first and foremost to this second kind of hoping. And so thanks to it we can take disappointments in our stride. The disappointments are of hopes of the other, lesser kind. And the loss of them can allow the deeper hoping to emerge. This has been shown to be true, apparently, in connection with the incurably ill. Once any hope of a cure has gone, there can emerge an inner freedom in relation to the illness concerned.

Disappointments allow for the purging of illusory hopes, and the emergence of the true hope. As Timothy Radcliffe pointed out, this was precisely the experience of the disciples of Jesus. "Are you going to restore the kingdom to Israel now?" And the answer was "no". The Kingdom is greater than you imagine. If we don't get what we want (because of other people, usually), we tend to sulk, get angry, become disaffected, separate ourselves etc. We have been deprived of a hope, an *espoir,* perhaps unfairly. But if we can let go of that, if we can say, It is good that you humbled me so that I may learn your commands, if we can commit our hope to God and leave it there, then the deeper *esperance* can well up in us.

Hope allows us to accept joys as well, to be "surprised by joy". In the particular joys that come our way, there is a foretaste of the immeasurable joy. And why should not God give us these? A recovery of health would be a humble example, but real enough, as we know from the Psalms and the Gospels. But so would, say, the touch of God in prayer, or good work that gives joy to oneself and others, or true friendship - the greatest human joy there is. Or, on a wider scene, the end of oppression, liberation from injustice. Christian hope knows that these things are not the ultimate coming of the Kingdom, but can welcome them wholeheartedly as penultimate signs of its coming.

We pray for hope

Here is a prayer for hope: "O Lord God, I hope by your grace for the pardon of all my sins and after life here to gain eternal happiness because you have promised it who are infinitely powerful, faithful, kind and merciful. In this hope I intend to live and die. Amen." That is the hope I have for myself. There's the famous prayer, "Order my loves within me." We could pray too, "Order my hopes within me": the coming of the Kingdom in oneself, the forgiveness of sins, holiness, purity of heart, the fullness of love, transformation in Christ, to be a Spirit-bearer. And nothing and no one can take that hope away from us. Except ourselves. But we can hope and pray that God will not allow that to happen.

Advent is a call to prioritise our hopes. If we hope supremely for anything else, we are simply buying ourselves a ticket to disappointment. And yet we know that "He who did not spare his own Son, but gave him up for us all, will he not also give us all things with him?" (*Rm* 8:32). And then of course the Holy Spirit will move us beyond ourselves. The more we love, the more we will hope for others, for our brethren and friends, for the Church, for the world.

"Hope, O my soul, hope." All the summonses of Advent go back to hope. Being vigilant in prayer, being patient, running to meet the Lord with good works. Hope makes us pray, makes us patient, makes us do things. And Advent ends not with a bang but a baby. As it's said, every birth is a sign that God hasn't given up on mankind. God hasn't given up hope in us. And our hope is a share in God's hope. Since Martin Luther King, people have been inclined to have dreams. So God has one too - for each and all of us. And despite all our kicking and screaming persists in it. So our hope, we can say, is a participation in his. But the child at the end of the tunnel of Advent is God's own child. Jesus is our hope.

Hope "sings the tune without the words". Perhaps we could say that Advent puts words to the tunes. It proclaims the divine promises. That's what the wonderful readings of Advent do too. They shower us with images of this unknowable thing. And surely the best way to move our souls to hope is to mull over these images. One could compose a beautiful litany of Advent from the prophets. A virtuous Branch for David, practising honesty and integrity in the Land, the Spirit resting on him; in those days Judah shall be saved and Israel dwell in confidence...the strong city, the mountain of the Temple lifted up and all the people streaming to it...swords turned into ploughshares...wolves living with lambs...the country filled with the knowledge of the Lord...a banquet of rich food, a banquet of fine wines... the wiping away of tears, the lifting of the mourning veil...justice for the downtrodden...the end of shame and guilt..."on the day the Lord dresses the wound of his people and heals the bruises his blows have left."

Advent - the Time of the Baptizer[1]

Mary and John: obedience and repentance

In a way, John the Baptist *is* Advent, just as, in another way, Mary is. Both of them, in complementary ways, prepared for the coming of Christ. Mary, as his mother, made his birth possible, his becoming one of us; she gave the Word flesh. John, as his herald, would baptize him thirty years later. He made his "epiphany", his public life possible. Mary stands for faith and obedience. "I am the handmaid of the Lord; let what you have said be done to me." John stands for repentance. "Repent for the kingdom of heaven is at hand." "Change your attitudes!" "Change how you live!" With Mary, Advent begins in a village, in a home, in the middle of daily life, where an angel finds her. With John it begins in the desert, away from the world. "The word of God came to John, son of Zechariah, in the wilderness."

Jesus never comes alone. He comes with the Father and the Holy Spirit. He comes with all the figures of the Old Testament behind him. He comes surrounded

[1] **(Sunday 2 Year C)** (*Ba* 5:1-9; *Ph* 1:4-6, 8-13; *Lk* 3:1-6).

by people: Zechariah and Elizabeth, Mary and Joseph, the shepherds and the wise men, Simeon and Anna, and John the Baptist. Later all the disciples. And the coming of Christ to us is the same. "Your friends are my friends", we say. This is why in our churches we have images and icons of the saints, and why in our calendar every year we celebrate Christ most of all, but so many others as well. And John the Baptist, the Bridegroom's friend, has a special place among them.

In the desert we meet Christ again

"The word of God came to John, son of Zechariah, in the wilderness." So let us go out to meet him.

I just want to focus on two things: the desert and the road.

The desert is John's place, the desert on the east side of the Jordan river. "Every truly new word, someone has written, begins in the desert, the uninhabited land where nothing is taken for granted and where nothing pretends to be what it is not. Before us we have arid land, the sky, a thin river, a powerful voice: that is all. The usual dwellings of men have been left behind, along with all the busyness and deceit of the world" (E. Leiva-Merikakis). This is where the word of God comes to John, this is where we have to go out to meet him and hear it. Aren't there deserts in us? If you were a Jew of John the Baptist's time, how full of meaning all this would have been! Leaving

Jerusalem, heading east, going down to the Jordan valley, over the river, into the wilderness. It was going back the way the Chosen People had come - first when almost 1500 years before they had come out of Egypt across the Sinai desert and then round through Transjordania, and again some 500 years before when they had come back from exile in Babylon.

In other words, going back to the desert was going back to the beginning. It was starting again, starting afresh. "In the beginning was the Word." It's through the Word the universe and the world come to be and continue to be. It was through the word of the covenant and Law Israel came to be. And now the word of God comes to John in the desert because the Word made flesh is on his way. And we can begin again. Isn't this what Advent's about? I think it's what this Year of Faith is inviting us to as well. To go back to basics, to faith, to the word of God, to the Gospel and the story of Jesus, to the living water of our baptism. And to make these things the basis of our lives, of our thinking and choosing and living.

A road for the exiles' return

And so to the road. "A voice cries in the wilderness: Prepare a way for the Lord, make his paths straight. Every valley will be filled in, every mountain and hill be laid low, winding ways will be straightened and rough roads made smooth. And all mankind - literally, all flesh - shall see the salvation of God." It's hard not to hear these words without hearing Handel's Messiah at the same time! They're the words of Isaiah originally. They were echoed in our first reading from the Prophet Baruch: "For God has decreed the flattening of each high mountain, of the everlasting hills, the filling of the valleys to make the ground level so that Israel can walk in safety under the glory of God." And now these words come into the Gospel and cry out to us. They're poetry. They're prophecy. But they're also down to earth. It's about building a road across the desert from Babylon, in modern-day Iraq, old Mesopotamia, to the Mediterranean coastal area of Palestine. A road for the exiles to return. A road that involves levelling the high ground, and filling in the low, then making sure it's straight and level. When you hear this, you could think of laying an airstrip in the Sahara or somewhere. And this airfield is for God to land on. This road is for us to come back to God, with God himself leading the way. "For God will guide in Israel in joy by the light of his glory", and through the desert of this life we have Christ, the Way, the Truth and the Life to follow.

"Prepare a way for the Lord." "What way shall we prepare for the Lord? A way by land? Could the Word of God travel such a road? Is it not rather a way within ourselves that we have to prepare for the Lord? Is it not rather a straight and level highway in our hearts that we are to make ready? Surely this is the way the Word of God comes in" (Origen). "Every valley will be filled, every mountain and hill be made low." Well, we all have valleys: our sadnesses and fear, our losings of heart, our little cowardices, our laziness. We all have hills: our pride, our self-importance, anger and impatience. In Advent the door of forgiveness is opened. It's a season for Confession. One day Aberdeen will have its Western Peripheral Route. This Advent we can listen to John the Baptist, that voice from the east, and lay a way in our lives for the Lord.

Advent - a time of the Holy Spirit

The spouse of Mary, preparing for birth

Isaiah, John the Baptist, Mary are the great Advent figures. They help us prepare for the coming of Christ. But there is Someone Else involved as well: the Holy Spirit.

The Holy Spirit *is* Advent, really. The Holy Spirit is the preparation. Mary conceives Jesus by the power of the Holy Spirit. We are reborn as children of God through the power of the Holy Spirit. There would be theologians and mystics who wouldn't hesitate to call the Holy Spirit the womb, the love, in whom the Father begets the Son and the Son is begotten. Christmas in any of its several senses is impossible, unthinkable without the involvement of the Holy Spirit.

Advent at one level is just four weeks of the Church's year. At another level, it contains at least four stories: of the physical universe and all humanity, of the Chosen People, of the Church awaiting the final Manifestation, of each human being on his or her way to rebirth in Christ.

Each of these stories is one of preparation, preparation for the birth of Christ, his birth in his own humanity in Bethlehem, in our humanity, in the whole cosmos. And the Holy Spirit is the hidden mover of these stories, the hidden historian.

It's a truism that the Holy Spirit has been the neglected person of the Holy Trinity. In the *Catechism of the Catholic Church* there was a real attempt to give a fuller portrait. One way this was done was by showing him always about four things, all in relation to Christ. According to para. 737, the Spirit *prepares* men for the meeting with Christ, he *manifests* Christ to them, he *makes* Christ *present* to them, and he *brings* them, through Christ, *into communion* with God. The liturgy of the Mass is the paradigm here. The Holy Spirit *prepares* us to meet Christ through the introductory rites which arouse repentance and faith. He *manifests* Christ to us in the liturgy of the Word, through the writings of prophets and apostles. He *makes* Christ *present* in his Paschal sacrifice through the consecration. He *brings us into communion* with the Lord when we eat his Body and drink his Blood. But, for the *Catechism*, the same four-fold activity of the Holy Spirit, which reaches its highpoint in the Mass, is going on in the whole of creation and the whole history of salvation.

God's yearning for the world's rebirth

Advent, we can say, contains especially the Holy Spirit's work of *preparation*. He prepares especially through the *prophets* of the Old Covenant. He "has spoken through the prophets," says the Creed. We can indeed think of all the inspired figures of the Old Testament who mediated God's Word to Israel. But we do inevitably think of the line of inspired speakers that began with Elijah, and then of the writing prophets, and then especially of Isaiah. In the prophets, humanity is offered the grace of contrasting itself inwardly with the entire universe, of rising above itself and the world. Reading Isaiah I think of the stanza of Edward Fitzgerald's *Rubaiyat of Omar Khayyam*:

> "Ah, Love! Could thou and I with Fate conspire
> To grasp this sorry Scheme of Things entire,
> Would we not shatter it to bits - and then
> Re-mould it nearer to the Heart's Desire!"

Prophecy is the very opposite of oriental or any other fatalism, it seems to me. It's the very opposite of the resigned acceptance of the status quo, of the way things are. Why has Western history been so full of utopian revolutions? It's thanks to the influence of Hebrew prophecy, however secularised. Oracles against Jerusalem and Judah, oracles against the Nations, oracles of judgement; oracles that predict precisely God's grasping of this sorry scheme of things and his shattering of it to bits. And then the re-moulding nearer to the Heart's Desire, the desire of the Heart of God. "Console my people, console them," says your God. Oracles of salvation, oracles of promise; a new heaven and a new earth, and a king who judges justly.

Through prophecy the Holy Spirit brings a "divine discontent" into the world. The "world" is such a power. It is so in possession. For myself, where I most felt that was Chicago: seen from the Lakeside. It was almost asking to be worshipped. The grace of prophecy is the grace to resist such idolatry, the grace to be able to contrast oneself inwardly with the world. And then not to turn to emptiness or nihilism, but to hope for a new heaven and a new earth.

Through the Holy Spirit, we recognise Christ

Let's take John the Baptist. He "was filled with the Holy Spirit even from his mother's womb." He *sees* the one on whom the Spirit rests, the Lamb of God who will take away the sins of the world. The Holy Spirit gives John the grace of recognition, of seeing Jesus. That is Christmas, very much.

There's that mysterious passage in Matthew 11: the question of John from prison. "Are you the One who is to come or are we to expect another?" If one takes the dark night of faith interpretation of this question, a temporary abandonment of John by the Holy Spirit (at least at the level of his consciousness), then think of the effect of Jesus's words, when they reached him. "Go and tell John what you see and hear etc." They would have been the all-illuminating flash of lightning in the dark. It was the reassurance of the Holy Spirit. And in the strength of that, John would have met his beheading with serenity, even though he did not live to see the Resurrection. And this too is part of the preparing work of the Holy Spirit: to be able to go on in darkness.

Another line: "The People of the 'poor' - those who, humble and meek, rely solely on their God's mysterious plans, who await the justice, not of men but of the Messiah - are in the end the great achievement of the Holy Spirit's hidden mission during the time of the promises that prepare for Christ's coming... In these poor, the Spirit is making ready 'a people prepared for the Lord' (Lk 1:17)" (*CCC* 716). The Holy Spirit, through the prophets and through the purifications of Israel's history, was preparing hearts for the coming of the Messiah. He was creating an empty space, poverty of spirit, purity of heart, a spiritual womb. Mary "stands out among the poor and humble of the Lord, who confidently hope for and receive salvation from him" (*Lumen Gentium* 55). This is a fruitful way of approaching the mystery of Mary's Immaculate Conception. Historians of the Judaism of Jesus's time stress how central to Jewish piety at this time was the desire for purity. In Mary, gratuitously and profoundly, the Holy Spirit brought this about. "The Holy Spirit *prepared* Mary by his grace...She was, by sheer grace, conceived without sin as the most humble of all creatures, the most capable of welcoming the inexpressible gift of the Almighty" (*CCC* 722). "In the fullness of time the Holy Spirit complete[d] in Mary all the preparations for Christ's coming among the People of God" (*CCC* 744). In her, Israel, and not just Israel, but the whole of creation, becomes what it is predestined to be: the seat of Wisdom, the place where his Glory abides. And it's the Spirit who does this.

He renews the face of the earth

All that is in the past, in one sense, and emphatically not in another. The Holy Spirit pursues his work of freeing people from the thraldom of the world, giving them a horizon of hope, unclenching fingers so that the hands are open to receive. The freedom to rise above ourselves, our circumstances. Hope, poverty of spirit, humility. The Holy Spirit is deftly, delicately leading people to faith in Christ and incorporation into his Body.

> "Since Christ died for all, and since all men are in fact called to one and the same destiny, which is divine, we must hold that the Holy Spirit offers to all the possibility of being made partners, in a way known to God, in the Paschal mystery" (*Gaudium et Spes* 22).

There is an action of the Holy Spirit in every life making possible a saving connection to the central event of salvation history: the death and resurrection of the Lord. "Even before Christ - *from the beginning*, throughout the world, this action has been going on," Pope John Paul added in *Dominum et Vivificantem*. "For this action has been exercised, in every place and at every time, indeed in every individual, according to the eternal plan of salvation, whereby this action was to be closely linked with the mystery of the Incarnation and Redemption."

At the same time, the Holy Spirit is at work in cultures and religions. "The Spirit, who 'blows where he wills', who 'was already at work in the world before Christ was glorified', and who 'has filled the world...holds all things together [and] knows what is said' leads us to broaden our vision in order to ponder his activity in every time and place." "The Spirit of God with marvellous foresight directs the course of the ages and renews the face of the earth" (*GS* 26). He "is at the origin of the noble ideals and undertakings which benefit humanity on its journey through history...It is the Spirit who sows the 'seeds of the Word' present in various cultures and customs." "He implants and develops his gifts in all individuals and peoples." "Every authentic prayer is prompted by the Holy Spirit." And so "the Church's relationship with other religions is dictated by a twofold respect: respect for man in his quest for answers to the deepest questions of his life, and respect for the action of the Spirit in man" (*Redemptoris Missio* 28-29).

This Spirit is the same Spirit "who was at work in the Incarnation and in the life, death and Resurrection of Jesus, and who is at work in the Church...Whatever the Spirit brings about in human hearts and in the history of peoples, in cultures and religions serves as a preparation for the Gospel and can only be understood in reference to Christ, the Word who took flesh by the power of the Spirit so that as perfectly human he would save all human beings and sum up all things" (*RM* 29).

The "hidden power"

As Advent approaches Christmas, everything more and more converges on a single point: the action of the Holy Spirit in the prophets, in John the Baptist, in Mary; the action of the Holy Spirit, in ways known only to God, in each individual; the action of the Holy Spirit in cultures and religions; the action of the Holy Spirit in the Church, in the Liturgy and the Eucharist; his action in our lives. This whole preparation "can only be understood in reference to Christ, the Word who took flesh by the power of the Spirit so that as perfectly human he would save all human beings and sum up all things".

The Holy Spirit - what a mystery, what a power he is! He's the real "hidden power", so much more powerful than the human wielders of what sociologists call "invisible power", more powerful than the powers of evil, "the spiritual hosts of wickedness in the heavenly places" (*Ep* 6:12). He is always at work, secretly converting, as in the past Israel, so now individual lives, historical movements, cultures, religions into Advents, into "wombs", into birth-places for Christ. May He be at work in us too, turning everything in us into a readiness to welcome the Lord!

Advent - God coming to birth in the world[2]

The eternal Son born as one of us

In a few days, the Church will celebrate the birth of the Saviour. The Church commemorates the events immediately preceding that birth. This means that she commemorates in particular his conception and hidden life in the womb of his virgin mother, Mary of Nazareth.

We believe that our Lord was not conceived in the ordinary way. He was conceived by a virgin and under the influence of the Holy Spirit. He had no human father. This is a truth of our faith and the truths of our faith are our food. We are meant to think reverently about them and pray about them.

Why, then, was our Lord conceived and born of a virgin? What does this extraordinary event signify? What does it say, what does it tell us?

It tells us, first, who our Lord is. Our Lord was conceived by a virgin because he was the eternal Son of God. He had no human father because he already had a divine Father. He already existed. He did not begin to exist

[2] (2 *S* 7:1-5, 8-12, 14, 16; *Rm* 16:25-27; *Lk* 1:26-38)

in Mary's womb. He already was, "in the beginning", with God the Father, a divine person, God from God, light from light, true God from true God. What happened in Mary's womb was that this divine Person, the Son of God, assumed - took to himself - added to himself - a human nature. He was already the Son of God as God. He now became the Son of God as man also. And this is the deepest truth about our Lord whether we think of him in his divine nature or in his human nature, that he is the Son of God. No, had he had a human father, this truth would have been obscured. Could Jesus as a man, Jesus who always stood in such a unique relation to his Father in heaven, who was indebted to Him and dependent upon his Father in every respect and delighted in revealing the fact, who surrendered himself entirely without reserve to his Father, who was always about his Father's business, could this Jesus have at the same time owed his existence to another father? Could he have had two fathers? We must say, no. We must say, that the one who was and is Son had to be conceived and born from a Virgin.

A new Adam is conceived

It tells us too that with the Incarnation God is beginning something new. God is involved in every conception. The parents are ministers of God. The child is the fruit of their action and God's action. Every human being begins in a special act of God. But here there is something more. "The Holy Spirit will come upon you and the power of the Most High will overshadow you." There is no human father. God is at the origin of this human being therefore in a unique way. God is, speaking humanly, intensely involved. We are reminded of the creation when the Spirit of God moved over the waters and life came. Now the same Spirit moves over a human virgin and something far more remarkable comes. "Therefore the child to be born of you will be holy." There is a new creation and the child in the womb is a new Adam, a new beginning for the human race, a gift from above, someone holy, someone who has not inherited the ancient sin, someone wholly penetrated by the Spirit and therefore able to give it to others.

Our Lord's virginal conception and birth tells us, lastly, what God will do for each of us. It tells us this particularly in the person of Mary - the virgin, the one who therefore was without a child, who had no achievement of her own, who was unfruitful. This virgin conceived and bore God. She became Mother of God. She was raised to the ultimate dignity.

But Mary is a type of the Christian, of us. "Christ has only one mother in the flesh, but we all bring forth Christ by faith." We all receive the Son of God. We all become God-bearers, Christ-bearers. We all become fruitful. The Holy Spirit descended on Mary at the Annunciation.

He descends on us at baptism. He forms Christ in us. He makes us sons of God and leads us to the Father.

Great things, then, great things happened in these months before the first Christmas. Great things happen now. God is present. God offers us wonderful things and will do them and does them. We only have to say yes - be it done according to your word - and surely that yes is worth saying.

Christmas - Midnight Mass

What a wonderful night this is!

It's light in darkness,
A virgin having a child,
A baby in a manger.
It's the son of David born in Bethlehem,
Wonder-Counsellor, Mighty-God,
Eternal-Father, Prince-of-Peace,
It's splendour on a hillside,
Angels singing to shepherds,
Glory to God and peace to men.

What a wonderful night this is!

Many aspects of Christmas can lose their charm for us, for whatever reason. But this story and its re-enactment in the Liturgy never does. It's fresh every holy night. Such is the power of the Holy Spirit.

Isn't it wonderful that, at the heart of our faith, there's a mother and a child? Who'd have thought that this is how God's grace would be revealed? It's so simple, so human, so divine. It wrong-foots all our pride. It subverts us. It takes us on the side we least expected to be taken. And yet it affirms us. It's God's "yes" to us beyond all our imagining. It's God taking us on, into himself, indissolubly and for ever.

How beautifully Isaiah anticipates this night: "the people that walked in darkness has seen a great light"!

How profoundly St Paul reflects on it: he goes to its heart, God's grace; he draws out its entailments for us, self-restrained, upright, prayerful living, with no ambition except to do good; he foresees its fulfilment, "the Appearing of the glory of our great God and Saviour Jesus Christ"!

Through my love, your history is transformed into God's way

And how unforgettably St Luke describes it!

"Caesar Augustus issued a decree." Caesar Augustus, no mean man, one of history's greats. He created a peace around the Mediterranean that would last more than 200 years, he created an Empire that would last in the East almost 1500 years and in the west, as the Holy Roman Empire, all the way to Napoleon. His age was an age of cultural flowering, military expansion, financial stability. He found Rome brick and left it marble. All credit to him! He was hailed as saviour, bringer of peace; he was even called divine. And he belongs to the past.

But the pregnant virgin on the donkey, the loyal fiancé by her side, and the child in the manger in the animals' cave just beyond the pub - they do not. They founded an Empire that will never pass away, because it's heavenly, not earthly, the Church of the living God. They live in the hearts and minds of millions of folk all over the world. They are even now comforting the homeless, the refugees, the little people, the living and the dying. They aren't myth. They aren't mere history. They're real. They're now. They're here.

Yes, tonight is a wonderful night.

"God's grace has been revealed",
"A child is born for us, a son given to us",
"In the town of David, a saviour, Christ the Lord".

Tonight is a wonderful night. It is "a sign for you", year after year, in difficulty or happiness, surrounded by a loving family or cold and lonely and afraid.

Tonight, the "jealous love of the Lord of hosts" says "Yes" to us, says to each and every one of us, "I love you." "I love you", not because you're handsome or beautiful or rich or powerful or clever or nice, but just because I do. Just because you are: man, woman and child, my precious human creation. I love you so much that, in my Son, I have become one of you. I will live and die like one of you. I will go down into your dark night and turn it into day. I love you, my precious human creation. I will take away your sin on the Cross and your suffering and death in my Resurrection. You will be mine and I will be yours, "and death shall be no more, neither shall there be mourning nor crying nor pain any more." "The jealous love of the Lord of hosts will do this."

"O sing a new song to the Lord,
Sing to the Lord all the earth.
O sing to the Lord, bless his name."

Tonight all this begins in Bethlehem. Tonight this love is unveiled, in the irresistible form of a baby. Tonight this love's goal rises in the night of our hearts and of our poor troubled world.

Tonight, already, we glimpse the light of everlasting day, and so we pray:

"O God, who have made this most sacred night radiant with the splendour of the true light, grant, we pray, that we, who have known the mysteries of his light on earth, may also delight in his gladness in heaven, who lives and reigns for ever and ever. Amen."

Christmas Day

I know an American gentleman who calls his house, "Love-in-the-ruins". I've never asked him why. But certainly it's not the kind of name you forget.

If you look at Renaissance paintings of the Nativity, often the stable is shown as dilapidated, ruined. It's a symbol, of course, of the world, of us. And there in the middle of the ruins is love; there is the Child.

And the readings we've just heard begin in the ruins. "Break into shouts of joy, you ruins of Jerusalem" (Is 52:9), said the first reading. Those words come from the sixth century B.C. Behind them lies the most shattering experience ancient Israel endured, and over which the Jews still grieve and fast today. This was the destruction of Jerusalem by the Babylonians in 586 B.C., when its walls, houses, palaces, and most of all, its Temple were all left in ruins. "The City where the most High dwells", the pride and joy of every Israelite's heart, the goal of his pilgrimages - in ruins.

It was all very real. But it's a symbol too, of the world, of us - like the tumble-down stable. We're in the stable; we're in the ruins. We can think of lives ruined by addiction to alcohol and drugs and other things. We can think that if a society can seriously contemplate same-sex marriage, then its idea of man and woman and marriage is surely in ruins. We can think of our broken families. We can think of our economic system. We can even wonder about the Church. And then about our own lives, and the dying that awaits us.

Beneath it all is the real ruin, the real gaping hole: our broken relationship with God. A fifth century Christian monk (John of Apamea) put it like this:

> "By growing away from the true God, our Father and Lord, humankind has become estranged from him. We have lost our sense of real life, squandered the treasures hidden within us, deprived ourselves of the knowledge of God, and have fallen into the deep darkness of ignorance ... incapable of [even] knowing ourselves."

Joy and consolation as he raises us up again

Yet, what Christmas says is that Love *is* in the ruins.

What the prophet Isaiah says is, "Break into shouts of joy together, you ruins of Jerusalem, for the Lord is consoling his people, redeeming Jerusalem" (Is 52:9).

What the Letter to the Hebrews is saying is that the word, through which God first made the house of the world we pull down around our ears, has now been spoken to it. Christmas is - to quote Karl Rahner - "God speaking his last, his deepest, his most beautiful word to the world: 'I love you, man; I love you, world.'"

Christmas is the apostle John solemnly proclaiming: "The Word was made flesh and dwelt among us. And we saw his glory, the glory that is his as the only Son of the Father, full of grace and truth" (Jn 1:14).

Love is in the ruins.

Yes, "the Word was made flesh" - our poor, ruined, smelly, mortal flesh - "and dwelt among us." "And to all who did accept him he has given power to become children of God" (Jn 1:12). He has restored that broken relationship, he has made us friends of God.

> "He has humbled himself, come down to us, put on our clothes of flesh, made himself visible. He comes and goes among us. He looks for us and finds us, while we are still in chains, miserable, corruptible, flat on the ground, sunk in deep darkness...He has stretched out his hand to guide us, taken hold of us and stood us on our feet again, restored our courage, given us back joy. He has saved and redeemed us, gathered us together and healed us. He has brought us peace, unity, purity, justification...He has drawn us to himself, united us with himself, reconciled us, made us share his grandeur, elevated us to his world of truth and his kingdom of peace...He is our hope, our expectation, our resurrection. He is beauty, clothing, glory, splendour, day, light, life, wealth and treasure" (John of Apamea).

No wonder that today Pope St Leo the Great could utter his memorable words: 'O Christian, be aware of your dignity - it is God's own nature that you share. Don't then by an unworthy way of life fall back into your former baseness. Think of the Head, think of the Body of which you are a member. Recall that you have been rescued from the power of darkness and have been transferred to the light and the kingdom of God."

So, my American is on to something: Love is in the ruins. God is with us. The Word has become flesh and lives among us. In every Eucharist, he is present, present in his flesh and blood, building up the ruins, turning our stables into temples of the Holy Spirit.

May we feel that this Christmas! May our friendship with God become closer, move to a new level! May we allow God's word and the grace of the sacraments to shape us and rebuild us and convince us of his love!

"A society begins to be decadent, it has been said, when everyone says to themselves, 'What's going to happen next?', instead of asking, 'What can I do?'" (Denis de Rougemont).

If Love *is* in the ruins, if God is with us, then there is something we can do. We can work with God - by purity of life, by everything we do at home, at work, anywhere, by our whole living and dying, by our prayer. We can rebuild the ruins in the power of his love. Amen.

Feast of St Stephen

A man alive in the Holy Spirit

Had any of us been asked what to celebrate the day after Christmas, it's unlikely we'd have suggested St Stephen. Suddenly we pass from the serenity of the stable to a furious theological argument that ends in someone being stoned and to a Gospel that tells us everyone will hate us. It seems a far cry from Bethlehem.

Yet throughout almost all of Christian history St Stephen has been celebrated precisely here: in the Eastern churches on the 27th December and among us today, the 26th. And this strange juxtaposition has proved to be full of meaning.

Who was Stephen, first of all? Let's attempt his personal profile. He was a leading figure in the Jewish-Christian community in Jerusalem in the years immediately after our Lord's death, resurrection and ascension. He's the first-named of the seven men proposed by the community and ordained by the apostles to distribute food to the needy - the seven men seen by Tradition as the first deacons. He was clearly an exceptional and Spirit-filled personality. "Full of faith and of the Holy Spirit," says St Luke, "full of grace and power". And he embarked on his mission with energy and success. He was a worker of "great wonders and signs", a gifted speaker: no one could resist "the wisdom and the Spirit with which he spoke". He was a man on whom the power of Pentecost had come to rest. And such are not usually left in peace. The Christians in Jerusalem were a new, growing group.

And as they grew so did tension with the Jewish authorities and their Council, the Sanhedrin. In the story of Stephen it reaches a climax. Previously the apostles had been *warned* against preaching that Jesus was the Christ. Then they had been *flogged* for doing so. And now Stephen is arrested, accused, brought before the Council and finally sent out of the city and *stoned*. "And that day a bitter persecution started against the church in Jerusalem", with Saul, who had approved Stephen's killing, a prime mover. But what is the upshot? The persecution compels the Christians to go elsewhere, and with them goes their message. The risen Christ changes Saul into Paul and sends him, not only to Jews, but to the Gentiles. The word of God passes beyond Jerusalem, out into the great wide Gentile, pagan, Greek and Roman world. Stephen's life and death was the turning-point that made all this possible, a bridge from the Church's Jewish beginnings to its Gentile future. In him, the proto-martyr, the famous words first came true, "the blood of martyrs is the seed of Christians".

A man radiating Christ

But to return to his arrest and trial and death. In the course of it, he's transfigured - something that has happened to others too. "His face was like the face of an angel," says St Luke. Against the garbled accusations thrown at him, he lays out the Christian position with considerable power, provocatively even. Anger rises against him. Proper judicial procedure seems to be set aside. But he "full of the Holy Spirit, gazes into heaven and saw the glory of God, with Jesus standing at the right hand of God." His passion has the form of Christ's. Like Christ, he's a subject of false accusations, undergoes a trial, stands firm. And he dies praying, praying to Jesus and praying like Jesus: "Lord Jesus, receive my spirit", "Lord, do not hold this sin against them." We catch the Gospel echoes. And out of this Christ-like passion comes the resurrection of the wider mission, the growth of the Church, the salvation of Saul. In the end, Stephen's profile is that of a disciple shaped to his Master.

> "I did not come to bring peace, but a sword." (Mt 10:34)

And so back to Christmas. The question is, what does this divine Child bring? St Stephen is an answer. It isn't the so-called Gospel of prosperity. It isn't an easy life. It isn't universal popularity. Today's Gospel could hardly be starker: "You will be hated by all men on account of my name." "You are well aware, then," wrote Paul to Timothy, "that anybody who tries to live in devotion to Christ is certain to be attacked." Persecution is woven into the history of the Church. It's a bitter part of the Church's present. The German bishops, for one, ask their faithful on St Stephen's day to remember the many Christians suffering for their faith now - in China, in India, in some Muslim countries and elsewhere. So it's something other than a comfortable life this Child has in his hand. It is something other and better. It's striking how often Luke uses the word "full" of Stephen. This is it: Jesus brings a fullness. In him all the fullness of God dwelt bodily, says St Paul, and of his fullness we have all received, says St John. Stephen is full of faith, says Luke. He's full of grace and power. He's full of wisdom. He's full of the Holy Spirit. These are charged New Testament words. They are different aspects of the fullness Jesus brings. They are namings of the grace of Pentecost, the fire Jesus came to cast on earth.

The gift of martyrdom

St Stephen is a sign, a "witness" (martyr), to this fullness. Thanks to this fullness he sees heaven opened and Jesus standing at the right hand of God. He sees the new closeness with God that Jesus brings. He sees his victory over death. And this turns the day of his death into a day of victory, a birthday into true and everlasting life.

And out of this fullness he can even pray, "Lord, do not hold this sin against them." Here is more victory. We won't all be martyred, but we do all get hurt, and hurt each other. Our natural instinct is to hug that hurt, and let it fill us, till we're full of resentment. Resentment is a cancer of the spirit. It's not what we're made for. No, it's not a comfortable life Jesus brings us. It's something other and better. It's the capacity to forgive and even ultimately forget. Saul and Stephen are friends now. It's the impossible the Christ Child brings, the unthinkable, a fullness that can even forgive the hurt. This is a gift so precious, so unique to Jesus, so quintessentially his, so at the very heart of the redemption he brings, that the day after his birth we celebrate someone who welcomed this gift to the full.

So we pray with Stephen, "Lord Jesus, receive my spirit." Receive it and fill it - not with me, but with your Spirit. Fill it with faith and power and wisdom and grace. Amen.

Mary, Mother of God

A Mother's heart ponders

"When the appointed time came,
God sent his Son, born of a woman..."

Today, it's this "born of a woman" that shines out. Today is the octave day of Christmas, the start of another year, and the solemnity of Mary, Mother of God. "Hail, holy Mother", says the Entrance Antiphon, "who gave birth to the King who rules heaven and earth for ever."

So let's follow the grain of the Liturgy and look at Mary.

"As for Mary," the Gospel says, "she treasured all these things and pondered them in her heart." Christmas was something Mary took inside herself and thought about. It engaged her memory: "she treasured all these things, all these words." She kept them, remembered them, didn't forget them. And they didn't just sit there, at the back of her mind, as it were. She "pondered them in her heart." Literally, "she threw them around", turned them over, mulled them over. She looked at them from different angles. She was trying with God's help to understand their meaning. She had a child in her arms and the words of angels and shepherds in her mind. And she wanted to put all this together. She wanted to make sense of it.

"As for Mary, she treasured all these things and pondered them in her heart." When I was a boy, these words intrigued me. And now what strikes me is just what an experience the first Christmas must have been for Mary. That's why she had to think about it. We don't know what she thought; it's her secret. But we can try and guess something of what she went through, something of what happened to her. I think St Luke, in the way he presents her, wants us to do this. And what strikes me again is how, moment by moment, scene by scene, everything in Mary is, so to speak, brought out by Christ, how her whole being rises up and becomes focussed and energised by him. It's the earth opening up in the face of heaven coming close.

Mary's whole being opens to God

Think back nine months to the annunciation. Here she is, a simple Jewish girl from an obscure village, going about her daily work. And suddenly she's greeted, fulsomely, by an angel. "Deeply disturbed", says St Luke, "she asked herself what this greeting might mean." She's already affected. He delivers his extraordinary message: she'll be the mother of the Messiah himself. Now her common sense asserts itself: "How is this possible if I'm a virgin?" He explains that a man won't be the cause but the Spirit of God - more extraordinary still. He assures her "nothing is impossible with God". And now the hidden grace in her speaks up. She gives her full consent to God's bewildering project and her own part in it. And she does indeed conceive by the Holy Spirit and become the Mother of God.

Think of this as an experience. Here's a human being, Mary, meeting the divine, and everything in her is involved, engaged, brought into play. Her femininity, the intimate parts of her body, all her chemistry, her emotions, her reason, her will, the hopes she shared with her people, her marriage-to-be with Joseph - it's all affected, touched, sparked. All of it wells up to meet the coming Christ.

Tenderness of a mother

Then go on through the Gospel. She visits Elizabeth. She wants to share her experience. She wants to help someone else caught up in the same story. And here still more emerges. When Elizabeth praises her she bursts out in praise of God. Her joy overflows. She sings the Magnificat. It's more of the human! Then she has her baby. She cuddles him, breast-feeds him, keeps him warm and dry, tickles him, rubs noses with him, makes funny noises back at him. She sings to him. There's a lovely carol *I heard an Infant weeping*. It has Mary singing a lullaby:

> My Lamb, from God forth-faring,
> My Life, my guiding Star,
> Fair Lily, of my bearing,
> Than jewel rarer far:
> Babe Jesu, lullaby!

Whatever, she was the real mother of a real baby. Then the shepherds come, and there are more strange angelic words to take on board.

These are just glimpses, flashes of what the Incarnation, the coming of Christ, meant for one human being, his mother. Enough of a flash I think to see that *everything* in her was affected. Every violin-string of her nature plucked and called upon to play. All her threefold potential - as a human being, a woman, a unique individual, as body, soul and spirit - elicited. And in time, not least, her capacity to suffer. She'd meet Simeon and Anna, hear that her son would be a sign of contradiction, and a sword pierce her heart. And indeed she'd have a three-day agony losing her boy in Jerusalem, she'd have the ultimate horror of watching him die on a cross. What was left of herself then? There's nothing in Mary, no corner of her, no aspect of her humanness, that wasn't taken up by Christ, emptied out and filled with Christ, given to Christ and the things of Christ. There was nothing in her outside her mission to be the Mother of God, and the Mother of the Church, the mystical Body of her Son. And there's nothing in her now, assumed as she is body and soul into heaven, outside his joy. It floods her. "My soul glorifies the Lord, and my spirit rejoices in God my saviour." "My Lamb, my Life, my Guiding Star, fair Lily of my bearing!" My pearl of great price. My treasure hidden in the field. My Jesus.

Mary's motherhood is for us too, enlivens us

And Mary's song, Mary's discovery, Mary's experience has the potential to be ours as well. Her son, God and man, is the one for whom the humanity of each and all of us has been waiting and in whom it is brought to birth. He is the One who makes us human, whom we were made and designed from all eternity to know, love, serve and be happy with for ever.

I might object: such passionate intensity is beyond me. Mary after all had a direct contact with Jesus, whereas my life, my body and soul, my emotions and thoughts and desires are all tied up, yes, in part with church and religion, but with other things as well: with family, with work, with friends, with worries over health and money and all the rest. But say that and we've missed the point. The point is, there is only one divine plan and it's for all of us. It's to bring together everything and everyone into Christ. This beloved baby body Mary holds in her hands is growing day by day into the mystical Body of the one same Christ. And all the people with whom our lives and emotions and thoughts are tied up are, potentially or actually, part of this body. So it *is* the same for us. Christ is everywhere and in everyone. He meets us in everyone and everything. And our whole life too, like Mary's, every nook and cranny of it, can, through the grace of the Eucharist and the power of the Spirit, be turned to him, engaged by him, taken hold of by him - through others for the most part. Our humanity too, as we live with and for each other, can be born and suffer and die and rise. Through him, with him, in him, it can realise its capacity for love. And this is what living really is.

When a Benedictine makes profession, he or she sings a Psalm-verse: "Receive me, Lord, according to your word, and I shall live. And you will not disappoint me of my hope." "Receive me. Lord, according to your word, and I shall live." Today's Collect calls Mary's son the Author of Life, its well-spring, its source. Let us, as this year begins, ask him to receive us - everything we have and are. Then we will live, as Mary did, as Mary does.

Epiphany

Wise seekers after God

"After Jesus had been born at Bethlehem in Judaea during the reign of King Herod, some wise men came from the east." So, after keeping Jesus's birth at Christmas, we remember these wise men at Epiphany.

They have always fascinated the Christian imagination, and they can fascinate ours. Probably they were astrologers and astronomers (the two things were not differentiated then). In our terms, a mixture of scientist and philosopher and religious inquirer. Probably they were from Babylon, in what is now southern Iraq, a centre for study of the stars. Perhaps the star they saw was an unusual conjunction of the planets Jupiter and Saturn in the constellation of Pisces which took place in the years 7-6 BC, now thought to have been the time that Jesus was born. And here's an interesting detail: the planet Jupiter was associated with the chief Babylonian god, Marduk, and the planet Saturn with the Jews. So if the two came together this would have been charged with significance. Certainly many non-Jewish people of the time knew the Jews were expecting a Messiah. There were still Jews in Babylon too. Perhaps the wise men were in conversation with them. Perhaps they heard of the prophecy of the Gentile Balaam in the book of Numbers: "I see him, but not now; I behold him, but not nigh: a star shall come forth out of Jacob and a sceptre shall rise out of Jerusalem." These are all real possibilities.

Whatever, these intrepid, pure-hearted magi "saw" and "went". They followed the star. They read the runes, as it were. They picked up the clues. They followed the trail and came with their gifts to worship the new-born King. In the Rule of St Benedict when a young person wants to enter the monastery, the first question he or she is asked is, "Are you really seeking God?" These men were. And they are patterns for us. They had a star in the sky. We have the star of faith. Their goal was Bethlehem. Ours is heaven.

Abundant fruits of the spirit

What a contrast Herod makes! He was "troubled", perturbed, "and so was the whole of Jerusalem". For him, the birth of the Christ was bad news, not good news. It was a threat to his own petty power, as the local big man. And isn't it strange that neither he, nor the chief priests and scribes, go on with the magi to Bethlehem? Beneath their dignity, I suppose. In fact, they dig themselves in. They stay where they are. They represent the world closed to what is above it. They knew their Bible, but they didn't seek God.

The magi did though. The star shone out again, and they were filled with delight. And on they went. These wise men were more than they realised. They carried more meaning than they knew. They were representative. They represent the world open to what's above it. They stand for science and philosophy and religion - human research, inquiry, wisdom - finding its way to Christ. They followed a star, their conscience. A hope for a better world drove them on. They were being guided more than they knew by the gentle Providence of God. Old prophecies were coming true in them. We heard one in the first reading: "[Jerusalem] the riches of the sea will flow to you, the wealth of the nations come to you; camels in throngs will cover you, and dromedaries of Midian and Ephah; everyone in Sheba will come, bringing gold and incense and singing the praise of God." Israel had long hoped that one day the Gentiles would turn to the God of Israel. In the magi this day dawns. And so they were carrying all of us, all the Gentile believers to come, who would make their way, generation after generation, to Bethlehem to worship the King of Israel. We come in their wake. And like them we too may be more than we realise. We carry the past and the future in us, and the more our lives move towards Christ, "to the beauty of your sublime glory" as the Collect calls it, the more the whole world is finding its bearings, coming right, fulfilling God's plan, making its way home. But Herod was troubled and he didn't move.

A new family, embracing all peoples

At Christmas Jesus is born. At the Epiphany the Church is born. At Christmas a person enters the world in a new way, God is made man, the God-man is born. At Epiphany, a new human family enters the world, a new social entity. Before there were the Jewish people on the one hand, the depositary of God's promises, and on the other the various scattered pagan Gentile peoples and nations, each going its own way. It was a divided world. But now, in the middle of it, a third, new thing appears: the Church, the extension of Christ through space and time. Here is the place where Jews and Gentiles can be reconciled, where "there is neither Jew nor Greek, neither slave nor free, neither male nor female, for you are all one in Christ Jesus" (*Ga* 3:28) and where the one true God is worshipped in spirit and truth.

In the second reading St Paul proclaims it: "the pagans now share the same inheritance, they are parts of the same body, and the same promise has been made to them, in Jesus Christ, through the gospel." Yes, he says, Gentiles and Jews are now coheirs, co-members, co-partners. The pagan wise men enter the house in Bethlehem and fall down before the Jewish boy on his mother's lap, and a new space, a new place, a new way of being human, and living with God and each other, opens up. It's a small seed of reconciliation and hope. It is the Church. It is Catholic unity.

The Epiphany calls us to open our heart

This is what Herod refused to accept, clutching his own little corner of power. This is the way the Jerusalem scribes, for all their knowledge, wouldn't go. And yet prophecy was fulfilled, and it is every day. "Though night still covers the earth and darkness the peoples", the "glory of the Lord rises" on Jerusalem, And at this sight, we, believing Jerusalem, should "grow radiant, [our] heart throbbing and full". The Epiphany calls us to open our heart: to the gift of God, the Incarnation of his Son, and the gift of one another.

So, here's a thought to end with, partly humorous, partly serious. The wise men have always sparked the imagination, as I said. In Jesus's time and long after, there were only three known continents: Asia, Africa and Europe. So perhaps, some have thought, one wise man came from Europe, one from Africa, one from Asia. This is why there's often a black king among them. And so it was the whole world, symbolically, that came to Bethlehem. Then think of the Bethlehem which is Aberdeen, the Church in this place, and Our Lady of Aberdeen and the kingly child she holds, with sceptre and crown. Don't we experience the Epiphany here?

Here over the last years have come people from Africa, Asia and the mainland of Europe: Africans with gold - the love of life and God; Indians and Filipinos with incense - prayer and spicy food; Eastern Europeans with the myrrh of a painful history and an embattled faith. Coming here to Jesus and Mary, to the Eucharist and the Church in this place.

Well, it's just a thought - and includes a grateful welcome to all from the Americas and Oceania! But we, we who got here first as it were, we must not be "troubled". Let our hearts be enlarged, as Mary's and Joseph's must have been by their exotic visitors. And let all of us, wherever we're from, let us allow the glory of God to open our hearts, in the great new space of the Church. Let us welcome one another. And with Mary and Joseph, angels and stars, shepherds and wise men, let us worship our God. He has appeared in the flesh, he is present in this Eucharist.

And then we will be stars to lead others to him.

Baptism of the Lord[3]

The Trinity reach into the depths to embrace us

Today is the last day and the last feast of the Christmas season - the Baptism of the Lord.

At Christmas, the Son of God eternally begotten of the Father is born in time of Mary his mother.

At Epiphany, the Church is born in the person of the Magi.

Today, each of us is reminded of our own rebirth by water and the Holy Spirit.

At the end of the Easter season, we have the feast of Pentecost. The Holy Spirit comes down in wind and fire. And at the end of the Christmas season, we have the feast of Christ's Baptism, when the Holy Spirit comes down on him in bodily shape, like a dove.

All four of the Gospels, each in its own way, mention that Jesus was baptised by John.

John's baptism wasn't our baptism. It wasn't a sacrament, though it was a step towards it. It was an outward sign of repentance. Centuries before the people of Israel had gone through the River Jordan to enter into their inheritance, the Promised Land. By going back to

[3] **(Year C)** (*Is* 40:1-5, 9-11; *Ti* 211-14, 3:4-7; *Lk* 3:15-16, 21-22)

the Jordan, they were expressing a desire to begin again, to be the people God wanted them to be.

And Jesus joins them. He wasn't a sinner; he's the Lamb of God who takes away the sins of the world. But he identifies himself with his sinful people. And he chooses a highly symbolic way of doing so. None of the Gospels directly mention this physical detail, but he must have *gone down* into the water. Off the bank into the river, and if it was high enough right under the water. He had already "come down from heaven", as the Creed says: not meaning a journey in space, but his becoming a human being. Now he goes still further down: into the muddy stream of sinful human history. And as we know, he was humbler yet, even to death on a cross, even to descent into the realm of the dead. Down, down, down he goes. And the Holy Spirit "descends" on him today, we hear. The Son *and* the Spirit, the two hands of the Father, go down together, down to us, down to all the lowest points - so that the Father can retrieve us, scoop us up, draw us back into his embrace.

This is the disconcerting revelation of a phil-anthropic (human-loving) God.

The radical cleansing of baptism

And this movement still goes on. By faith, baptism, sanctifying grace, Jesus is born and appears and comes down in each of us. He comes down to our level. He lives his life with each and all of us. The Fathers of the Church love to say that today Christ purified, consecrated water, and so inaugurated the sacrament of baptism. We can enlarge that a little. Human history is the water. Our own lives are the water. They flow, they pass. Sometimes our water is muddy, sometimes turbulent. Sometimes it runs low, a mere trickle, sometimes, like the river at Stonehaven, it overflows and spreads mud and mess everywhere. But down into this water comes the Spirit-bearing Christ. He purifies it, consecrates it. He enters its flow. He makes it a source of life for others. He changes it into a river of life that will flow, not like the Jordan, into the dead end of the Dead Sea, but into the ocean of God's enthralling, all-encompassing, life-giving infinity.

We live our lives. We have our family life and our work and things to do. We marry or we don't or we did once. We have children or we don't. We're in good health or we're not. But here's the wonder: into all of this Christ comes. He doesn't take it away. He purifies it. He pours into it faith, hope and love. He gives, broadens and deepens our life. He fills the ordinary daily things with meaning and grace and prayer. After his baptism, Jesus is praying, says St Luke. And so in us. The heavens are opened: the relationship with God clouded over since the sin of Adam is now possible again. Everything good we do, not just the holy things but each and every thing, can be worship of God. The Holy Spirit comes down, and the Father speaks: "You are my Son, the Beloved; my favour rests on you." Every day the Father says that to each of us.

All this is the grace of Baptism.

God waits for us as the new year unfolds

Christmas, Epiphany, the Baptism of the Lord. These are wonderful feasts. "God's grace has been revealed," says St Paul, "and it has made salvation possible for the whole human race." And isn't it a nice touch that the Church's year begins just a little before the Civil year? Before the New Year is born, Christ is born, and when it has just been born, we're reminded that we have been re-born: "justified by grace." So it's God who leads, God who starts the sentence, God who tells the story, not the world. "Console, my people, console them, says your God. Speak to the heart of Jerusalem and call to her that her time of service is ended, that her sin is atoned for...Here is the Lord coming with power...He is like a shepherd leading his flock." He goes first. If we've lived this Advent and Christmas well, if we've renewed our sorrow for our sins and received the gift of forgiveness once again, if we've felt our faith revived, what a good position we're in to begin another year. We've stolen a march on the Evil One. The life-giving water of Christ is already flowing in our lives.

Who knows what lies ahead of us this year? But what we do know is that God is there already. God is with us. Christ is in us. The Holy Spirit is over us. And the motherly prayers of Mary are around us.